TELL ME MORE! science

Why do birds have
FEATHERS?

by Ruth Owen

Ruby Tuesday Books

Published in 2021 by Ruby Tuesday Books Ltd.

Designer: Emma Randall
Editor: Mark J. Sachner
Production: John Lingham

Photo credits:
Alamy: 6 (top), 18–19; FLPA: 14–15; Nature Picture Library: 10, 17; Shutterstock: Cover, 1, 4–5, 6 (bottom), 7, 8–9, 11, 12–13, 16, 18, 20–21, 22, 23.

Library of Congress Control Number: 2020946826
Print (hardback) ISBN 978-1-78856-177-8
Print (paperback) ISBN 978-1-78856-178-5
eBook ISBN 978-1-78856-179-2

Printed and published in the United States of America
For further information including rights and permissions requests, please contact: **shan@rubytuesdaybooks.com**

Contents

Fantastic Feathers

Birds are the only animals with feathers.

Their feathery covering protects them from thorns, insects, hot sun, wind, rain, and snow.

Flight feathers

Body feathers

Tail feathers

A macaw parrot

A bird moves its feathers as it flies or when it shows off.

It may pull them close to its body to keep warm.

The feathers are attached to tiny **muscles** that allow a bird to move them.

Feathers are made from keratin. It's the same stuff that your hair and nails are made from.

Tiny feathers

How Do Feathers Grow?

When a chick hatches, it has a covering of tiny, fluffy feathers called **down**.

Down

Cockatiel chick

After a few days, tiny spikes sprout from the chick's body.

Each spike is a new feather that's rolled up like a tiny tube.

Spikes

Soon the feathers begin to uncurl from the tips of the tubes.

Tube

Tip of new feather

The feathers on a bird's body are called contour (CON-toor) feathers. Under the contour feathers are tiny, soft, down feathers that keep the bird warm.

If you want to see an adult cockatiel, turn to page 23.

Feathers for Flying

The big stiff feathers on a bird's wings help it fly.

As a bird flaps its wings downward, they force the air down.

This pushes the bird up.

Then the bird flaps its wings upward, and they are ready for the next downward movement.

The bird's wings also push the air backward, which pushes the bird forward.

A bird changes direction by moving its feathers to change the shape of its wings. By tilting a wing down, it turns to that side.

Feathers for Hiding

The colors and patterns on a bird's feathers can be good **camouflage**.

Golden plover birds lay their eggs in nests on the ground.

The chicks' feathers help them hide from **predators** in the plants around their nest.

A screech owl's
feathers blend
into a tree's bark.

Screech owls sit perfectly
still on a branch or in a tree
hole. Their camouflage
hides them from bigger
owls, mink, and other
hungry predators.

Feathers for Survival

Emperor penguins live in Antarctica, where temperatures can drop to -40°F (-40°C).

To survive the extreme cold, emperor penguins have a covering of 30,000 **waterproof** contour feathers.

Under this outer layer are up to 150,000 **insulating** down feathers.

Chick

Emperor penguins hunt for fish in the freezing ocean. Sometimes they dive up to 1,600 feet (488 m) beneath the icy water!

Feathers for Showing Off

When the mating season comes around, male ruff birds gather in a group called a lek.

The males show off to attract a female **mate**.

They bow and jump and flutter their wings.

A ruff bird

They also fluff up the large ruffs of feathers around their necks.

Ruffs live in **marshes** and on the shores of lakes. They are wading birds that wade in shallow water hunting for insects, small fish, and frogs.

Feathers for Carrying Water

Sandgrouse are birds that live in dry, desert-like places.

When sandgrouse chicks need a drink, the father bird flies to a **waterhole**.

He sits in the waterhole and shakes his belly feathers so they soak up water.

Father

Mother

Chick

Then the sandgrouse flies back to his family.

The chicks gather around their dad and drink the water from his feathers.

A sandgrouse's feathers can soak up about two tablespoons of water.

Father sandgrouse collecting water

Feathers for Singing

To attract a mate, a male club-winged manakin bird sings to females.

He does this by using his wings like a musical instrument.

He raises his little wings above his back.

Then he shakes the feathers back and forth—100 times a second!

The feathers rub together and make a loud *tick ting, tick ting* sound.

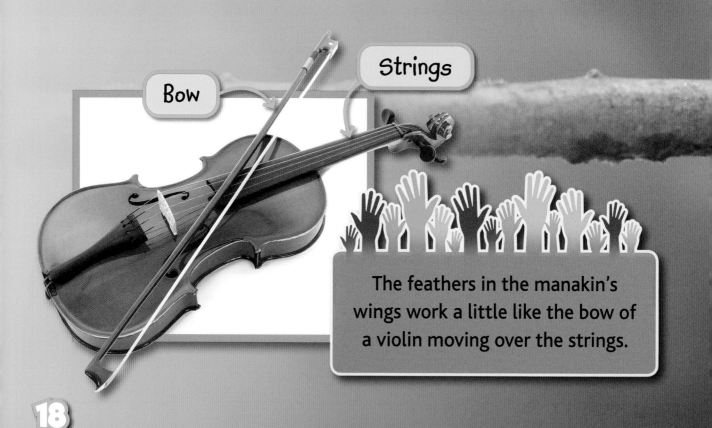

Bow

Strings

The feathers in the manakin's wings work a little like the bow of a violin moving over the strings.

New Feathers

Have you ever seen a bird that looks bald or scruffy? What's going on?

A bird's feathers get old and damaged.

So once or twice a year, most birds **molt**.

Some or all of a bird's old, worn feathers fall out.

A northern cardinal molting

Then, over a couple of weeks, a set of new feathers grows.

Sometimes a bird loses a single feather. Then a new one starts to grow back immediately.

A northern cardinal taking a bath

Let's Talk

Which feathery fact did you like best? Why?

Let's Investigate Feathers

A feather has a center stem called a rachis (RAY-kiss). Parts called barbs grow from the rachis. Tiny, hooked parts called barbules grow from the barbs.

Barbules with hooks

Barbs

Zipped up

Unzipped

Rachis

The barbules hook together to keep a feather smooth. It's a little like closing a zipper.

If the barbules come unhooked, the feather isn't smooth. It may let water through to the bird's body or affect the bird's flight.

Birds rearrange their feathers with their beaks to keep them smooth. This is called preening.

Check Out a Feather

1. Find a feather in a backyard or park.

2. Move your fingers gently over the feather. Can you unzip it?

3. Now try preening the feather with your fingers. Can you zip it back up?

4. Always wash or sanitize your hands after touching bird feathers.

An eagle preening its tail feathers

Glossary

camouflage
Colors, markings, or body parts that help an animal blend into its habitat.

down
Soft, fluffy feathers. Chicks have down when they hatch. Adult birds also have down under their outer feathers.

insulating
Able to keep out cold or keep heat in.

marsh
An area of land where the ground is always very wet and there are ponds, lakes, and streams.

mate
An animal's partner with which it has young.

molt
To lose feathers or fur to be ready to grow a new coat.

muscle
A part of an animal or person's body that moves bones. A bird's muscles also move its feathers.

predator
An animal that hunts and eats other animals.

waterhole
A hole in the ground that holds water that usually comes from rain. Animals drink at waterholes.

waterproof
Able to keep out water.

Adult cockatiel

Index

Read More

Boothroyd, Jennifer. *Feathers (First Step Nonfiction – Body Coverings)*. Minneapolis, MN: Lerner Publishing Group (2012).

Owen, Ruth. *Wings, Paws, Scales, and Claws: Let's Investigate Animal Bodies (Get Started With STEM)*. Minneapolis, MN: Ruby Tuesday Books (2017).

Answers

Page 13:
A scientist named Cassondra Williams wanted to learn how emperor penguins survive in Antarctica. Cassondra carefully studied the bodies of four penguins that had died. She observed and recorded 12 different kinds of feathers on the penguins' bodies. She also counted the feathers!